Maxi's Story

Beverly Kuzman

Sarasota, Florida

Graphic design by Rebecca Barbier.

For information regarding permission,
call 941-922-2662 or contact us at our website:
www.peppertreepublishing.com or write to:
the Peppertree Press, LLC.
Attention: Publisher
1269 First Street, Suite 7
Sarasota, Florida 34236

ISBN: 978-1-936343-27-0

Library of Congress Number: 2010932904

Printed in the U.S.A.

Printed August 2010

Dedication

To the organizations and groups who are working for the welfare of all of our furry friends, just like Maxi.

Chapter One

Maxi Joins Our Family

"There's a dog sitting along the road. He was there yesterday and he is sitting in the same place today," my husband said when he returned from a trip to buy groceries.

It was early March in Wisconsin and patches of ice still dotted the roadside. Nights dipped below freezing. This was not a time for a dog to be outside without any shelter.

"I'm going to take him some food and water. Do you want to come along?" my husband continued.

There was no doubt. Of course, I'd go along. From the time I'd been a young child, I had collected all kinds of injured or orphaned animals. When neighbors had piglets that were runts or injured and wouldn't survive without special care, they'd call, knowing that I would bottle feed them. We'd had raccoons, skunks, rabbits ....

We drove back the quarter mile and stopped near the dog. He stood up and looked at us, but it quickly became apparent that we were not the people he had hoped to see. He ate the food and then sat back down to wait. We were convinced that he believed that whoever had left him would return, so he didn't dare leave the spot for fear of being missed.

We didn't know what to do, but this dog had waited at least 48 hours for someone to return for him. He didn't deserve to be left on his lonely vigil any longer. We couldn't coax

him into our car, so my husband walked with him to our home, all the while urging him to abandon the spot where he had waited so patiently.

He was medium sized, about 35 pounds packed into a study body. He had a very dense, rough coat, which undoubtedly helped him survive the freezing nights. We later learned that he was at least part red heeler, dogs that are often used around cattle as herding dogs. We knew he was here to stay. How could we not give a home to a dog that was so loyal that he'd sit waiting for whoever had dumped him for two days and two even colder nights?

We fed him and made a bed for him in the corner of our garage, but our big concern was how he would be accepted by Spinner, our male Jack Russell Terrier, who had been the only dog in our household for over seven years.

Chapter Two

Spinner, Meet Your New Brother

For those of you who are not familiar with the Jack Russell Terrier as a breed, it might be of interest to know a little about them. The breed was developed to hunt small game. They are tenacious. The Jack Russell can best be described as a little dynamo on legs.

When Spinner first became a member of our household, I was amazed at his non-stop energy for playing. He played with his tennis ball for hours. We'd throw it, he'd bring it back. We'd throw it. He'd bring it back. If we stopped playing, he would shove the ball into our hands.

Some Jack Russells can be "snappy" and/or "yappy." Spinner was neither. In his 13 years with us, I never heard him bark. He was even-tempered and loving. His name was a perfect choice for him. Whenever he was happy, he would spin … and Spinner seemed to believe that life was a big circus and his act was to spin and spin.

I am also convinced that he had a sense of humor. When unsuspecting guests would leave their luggage open, he would make a raid on the open suitcase. He would take underwear out and race through the house with the garments.

In one case, he left a trail of women's panties leading from the guest room to the living room. He never did any damage to the items, but I instinctively knew that these items—

he never took any others—would cause laughter. Probably his laid-back, happy-go-lucky personality made the addition of a new dog to our household easy.

The two dogs forged an immediate friendship. Even though the new dog was larger than Spinner, Spinner was the one in charge. He took his new companion on a tour of our 23 acres, showing him some of his own favorite spots. They played endless games of tug-of-war, with Spinner's tenacity evening out the new dog's weight advantage. They often went down to our six-acre spring-fed pond and watched the fish in the water.

They became instant buddies.

Chapter Three

Every Dog Needs a Name

We couldn't continue to call him, "The Dog by the Side of the Rod." He needed a name. Some dogs are named for their lineage. Since we had no idea of our dog's background, that wouldn't work. Some dogs are named for their personalities. Spinner is a perfect example of that, but we really didn't know anything about our new addition, except that he would receive a "10" if he was being rated for his loyalty. Since he wasn't a puppy, he had to have been called something in his past life. We thought if we could find a sound that he responded to, we could use that as a basis for his name.

My two nieces and my sister-in-law were visiting. Taking turns, we would call out a name and watch for a reaction.

"Skippy," "Jack," "Riley," "Pooch," "Dog." But he reacted to none of these. "Target," "Rex," "King," "Laddie," "Brutus." Again, no reaction, so we tried again.

"Judge," "Schatze," "Ginger." But he only looked puzzled.

We decided that we would each suggest a name and then vote on our suggestions. The one receiving the largest number of votes would be his name.

"Buddy," "Baxter," "Joey," "Max," and "Bingo." The only name that received two votes was "Max." So now "The Dog by the Side of the Road" was officially christened, "Max." It was only a short time before he became "Maxi."

Chapter Four

A Trip to the Vet

I made an appointment with our vet for 2 P.M. the following day. Fortunately, I started early or we would have been late.

Maxi could not be convinced to get into our truck. I thought that Spinner's happiness at being included in this trip would lure Maxi into the truck cab, but Maxi would come to the open door, put his front feet on the door frame and then freeze into place, becoming an unmoving ice sculpture. I thought the memories of his last ride, when he had been deserted on our road, made it impossible for him to voluntarily join Spinner and me.

Would a food treat be enough to get him into the truck? There was leftover steak from last night's dinner, so I ran into the house to get it. But Maxi was steadfast and refused the bribe. Spinner happily ate the steak. Maxi was still outside the truck.

My next idea was to lift Maxi in, quickly close the door and run around to the driver's side. I later found that Maxi topped the scale at 36 pounds, but lifting a dog that suddenly seemed to have at least 10 legs, each struggling to brace him from being put into the Dodge Dakota, was much harder than I had anticipated. "Maxi, look! Spinner is in the truck. You'll like it," I pleaded.

Maxi was unmoved by my pleas. He remained an unmoving ice sculpture. Twenty minutes had passed and we were no closer to being loaded than when we first began.

Okay, let's move on to Plan D! I thought I'd try to load Maxi from the driver's side. "Maxi, come here," I intoned. Maxi joined me immediately and seemed happy to be able to do at least one thing I requested. I opened the door and again picked up the dog, who now seemed to weigh no less than 50 pounds with at least 15 legs, each of which seemed to be going in different directions. "See Spinner," I said to Maxi. "Look, Spinner loves the truck and you will, also."

Finally, I had Maxi on the seat, but that left little room for me. "Move over, Maxi. See Spinner, go see Spinner." This dog with 15 legs obviously suffered a hearing loss. "You can't drive, Maxi. Move over NOW." As this point, 35 minutes had passed since I had made my first attempt at loading Maxi. I went over to the passenger side, climbed in and tried to pry the now 70-pound dog from behind the steering wheel. It took only another five minutes to dislodge the determined dog from the seat.

We still had 20 minutes to drive the five miles to the vet. No problem. We'd gone about a mile when I heard Maxi vomiting. Oh, well, we can clean that up once we reach the vet.

The remainder of the ride was uneventful. Although Maxi didn't seem to be looking out the windows, when we crossed the Pecatonica River with its covered bridge, he ducked as low as he could go, obviously believing that we'd all be beheaded otherwise.

We pulled in to Dr. Dodge's parking lot with five minutes to spare. Of course, I hadn't counted on Maxi's new attitude. He had survived the truck ride, had made it past the beheading bridge, and he's now decided he had no intention of leaving the truck.

Pleading with him did not change his idea that the truck was now a refuge. He obviously intended to spend the rest of his life within the loving arms of the blue Dodge Dakota.

"Get out, Max! See, Spinner will get out." He paid no attention to me. His hearing loss had returned, but I was getting better at removing the ice sculpture. I finally had Maxi in my arms outside the truck. Spinner seemed to be puzzled by our new games, but thankfully, he was willing to get back in the truck.

"Okay, Maxi, if your legs are now paralyzed, I'll carry you into the office." We reached the door, but I couldn't open it with my arms filled with 36 pounds of quivering dog. I knew someone was bound to come out and that would give us a chance to stagger into what Maxi must have thought were the jaws of a monster. It must have been only a minute or two, but it seemed much longer. I was getting tired and just a bit annoyed with the entire affair.

Once in the office, I knew we'd have to wait since there were several people sitting in the chairs ringing the room. Incidentally, all of them had dogs on leashes and all their dogs were sitting calmly beside them. There was a sign on the wall asking people to keep their dogs under control. That was not a concern for me since I was holding my 36-pound bundle of quivering jello on my lap. Although it is not unusual to see small dogs sitting on their owners' laps, this may have been a first for the other waiting dog owners, a burly, relatively large dog, perilously perched on a woman's lap.

When our turn came, it was a relief to put Maxi on the examining table and into someone else's hands.

Dr. Dodge took a history, but since I knew nothing about Maxi's background, she made an educated guess at Maxi's breed and age. Dr. Dodge said that Maxi was two years old and at least part Australian Cattle Dog. She explained that dogs of this breed were either black/grey or red, as Maxi was.

She said they were sturdy, generally fearless working dogs and good around cattle and other farm animals. Maybe Maxi was fearless around cattle, but he certainly would not qualify as "fearless" around beheading bridges or killer trucks.

Maxi was given the necessary shots and fortunately would not have to return for two years. Now I only had to load him into the truck and navigate the dangerous five miles home!

CHAPTER FIVE

Special Delivery

We were all outside working in the garden. My husband and I were weeding and the dogs were randomly digging with occasional breaks for a quick game of tug-of-war. Today they had a rope, but often, they used a sock that had very little chance of surviving the game.

We saw our mailman, Greg, turn into our driveway and drive up to the house, which he did when there was a package or something that needed a signature.

We, all four of us, went over to the car and Greg said we had a package. He held out a very young puppy. He explained that when he opened our mailbox, the puppy was inside. Although we had to laugh, this was a really cruel, heartless thing to do … on a par with Maxi's dumping. What if we hadn't had any mail today? Greg wouldn't have stopped and the poor puppy would have died in the metal mailbox when the sun beat down on it.

What was next? We already had two dogs and numerous cats. We positively did not need another dog. I reminded my husband that one of our neighbors had stopped and asked if we had seen their dog, which had vanished. If they had not found their dog, maybe they would be willing to take the puppy. Otherwise, we would have to take a trip to the one no-kill shelter we knew about. But I knew they wouldn't take a puppy this young, which would

mean we'd have to keep it for a month … and I knew that was dangerous. How could you not fall in love with a puppy?

I kept repeating to myself, "We do not need another dog. We do not need another dog." We already had one dog that never wanted to quit playing and another dog that was neurotic and eccentric. "We do not need another dog."

But in this case, Fortune smiled on us. Since our neighbor's dog had not returned, they were willing to take delivery of our "Special Delivery."

Chapter 6:

Is There a Sign over Our Property?

With the steady stream of "drop-offs," we became convinced that there must be a sign over our property advertising an animal shelter. A mother dog and a puppy strolled up our driveway. We never knew where the mother went, but the puppy stayed. By this time, we knew the route to the no-kill shelter perfectly. The puppy was just the right age to be readily adopted. Whenever we took an animal to the shelter, we felt we should make a donation to help with the costs of care. It was both time-consuming and expensive, but we are firm believers in no-kill shelters.

Our property had four outbuildings. These buildings had been used to store hay, straw, and farm-related materials. They became perfect refuges for the cats that appeared … and perfect homes for the explosion of kittens. We knew we had to do something to control the cat population.

This was one activity in which Maxi and Spinner could not be involved, because the kittens would scatter at the sight of the dogs. When we think of kittens, we think of playful, sweet little fur balls, eager to be petted. These kittens, never handled by humans, were wary, wild and mean. If caught, they scratched, bit and howled as though they were being tortured. When this happened, all the other kittens would then vanish.

My plan was to let the kittens get used to me. I took a chair out to the building where

most of the kittens could be found. I talked to them. I sang to them. I read to them. As they became used to having me around, they would start reappearing. I brought dishes of food, which I'd place close to me. If I was quiet, I'd be joined by a bevy of kittens.

I wore long leather gloves. I had learned from experience that bare hands didn't work, and I had the scratches and bites to prove it. I had a tall box to put a captured kitten in and a cover that was heavy enough to keep my unhappy guest inside. It didn't take very long before I'd captured a kitten, but the kitten's noisy outrage meant all the other kittens went into hiding.

We would make a one-kitten trip to the shelter. We were delighted when we once made a two-kitten trip after an unusually successful kitten-capture day. I was able to catch and relocate all the kittens, but we knew it would only be a short time before new batches of kittens would appear unless we neutered the mothers.

By this time the adult cats, which all seemed to be female, were friendly. They would line up, along with Maxi and Spinner, to take turns being combed so we knew that catching and taking them to Dr. Dodge would be relatively easy. Since we had two cat carriers, it seemed logical that two cats would go at a time. We would only need to make three trips to complete the neutering.

I think I first heard the word, "CACOPHONY," when I was in high school and I had always felt it was a wonderful word that clearly sounded like what it meant. And there is no better word to describe the five-mile trip to Dr. Dodge with the two very unhappy and angry cats. Big Mama and Black Tail must have made enough noise to be heard in the next county. "Cacophony" without a doubt! … And I thought Maxi's trip to the vet had been stressful!

Two down! Only four to go …

Chapter Seven

Lessons

To make life go more smoothly, there were a few basic lessons Maxi needed to learn: walking on a leash, coming when called, and riding in a car. I soon learned that there were at least two ways to do things, my way and *Maxi's* way.

Maxi was an eager student. If we had been in a classroom, he would have been the one emptying the pencil sharpeners or passing out papers. He really wanted to please me.

We had a long driveway and it was a perfect place to learn to walk on a leash, since there was no other foot or vehicle traffic. Even though Spinner had learned these things long ago, he was always a part of Maxi's lessons. So we were ready to start. Maxi was on a leash on my right and Spinner on my left. We managed to get about three feet down the driveway before Maxi decided that it would be more fun if he and Spinner were walking together.

It only took me several minutes to untangle the leashes and we were off again, this time with Maxi on my left and Spinner on my right. Now Maxi decided that he really did prefer walking on my right. Circling behind me, he joined Spinner who now had decided that it was more fun to also switch sides. The three of us were tangled again. We had managed to go at least five feet. At this rate, we might be at the end of the driveway by sunset.

But Maxi had a solution. He took the end of his leash in his mouth and walked along beside us. As I said, there was my way and there was Maxi's way.

Having had many dogs in my lifetime, I had never had one that didn't like to ride in the car, so I was convinced that with practice, Maxi would learn to like riding in a car.

I decided that every afternoon, Maxi, Spinner and I would take a short ride in the truck. I had learned how to get Maxi in the truck cab. He did want to go along, so he would put his front feet on the side of the open doorway. Coming up behind him, I would lift his back legs and give a quick push. And, almost like magic, Maxi was loaded.

We turned left as we exited our driveway and drove up the small hill on Dunbarton Road. We reached the top, had gone about a quarter of a mile, and Maxi vomited. Not one to give up after just a little setback, we continued the lessons, always with the same result. If I were to rate the effectiveness of Maxi's car riding lessons on a scale of #1 to #10, maybe when I'm in an optimistic mood, it might be a #2.

One time when Fran, one of Maxi's favorite visitors, was spending a few days with us, we decided that we'd go to dinner at a restaurant in a small town about five miles from our home. Spinner was going along, but because of Maxi's reaction to car rides, he was going to stay home.

We turned up Dunbarton Road and had gone a short distance, when Fran told me to stop. Maxi was running alongside the road parallel to our car. We stopped, Maxi came over to us, and if a dog could smile, Maxi was … it was as though he were saying, "See, I can go with you!" We waited while my husband walked Maxi back home.

Chapter Eight

Shoes, Where Are My Shoes?

It isn't unusual for dogs to collect things. Some dogs like toys, some like bones. Spinner loved balls, but Maxi loved shoes.

Maxi didn't chew on shoes or destroy them. Maxi just collected shoes.

If you visited us and left your shoes at the door, quite possibly when you left, you might only find one shoe or if Maxi had been really busy, no shoes. The first place we'd look for the missing footwear was in Maxi's bed. At one time, I counted 12 shoes in Maxi's bed.

In case your shoes weren't in Maxi's bed collection, the next place to look was the field or the garden. However, there was a slight problem with the field collection of shoes. In case of rain or snow, the shoes were still in the field. Maxi's shoes only went one way—there was never a return trip.

Chapter Nine

Those Pesky Moles

Moles can do major damage to lawns or gardens. Moles are small, less than a foot long, with spade-like front feet. It is hard to believe that they could do so much damage, but as you drove down the roads of Lafayette County, you could see beautiful green lush lawns that were scarred by piles of dirt and raised tunnels. These areas might cover a six-foot square area.

Every hardware store, every garden supply store, and every farm supply store sold products that were guaranteed to rid lawns of moles. You just needed to follow directions, keep your fingers crossed and hope that your moles were not too wise to fall prey to these products.

But all the products sold were not as effective as Maxi and Spinner. The two dogs were expert mole exterminators. They walked around the lawn with their heads cocked, listening for mole sounds. Whatever sounds moles make could not be heard by humans, but Maxi and Spinner could hear the moles at work. Maxi would dig until he found the offending mole, toss it to Spinner, who then shook it until its tunneling days were over. Whenever I saw them at work or saw the result of their mole removal system, I would praise them extravagantly.

One day when I was reading on the deck and the dogs were playing, Maxi came up to me and laid an adult raccoon at my feet. The raccoon and Maxi were both soaking wet. He must have caught it in the lake and he also must have felt that if I was so excited over a little

mole, this new present would make me ecstatic. How could I explain that bigger was not necessarily better …?

Maxi and Spinner could have started a mole removal business. There would just be one major problem. They could only work at places they could walk to, since Maxi had problems with riding. Their business would never go international!

CHAPTER TEN

Patches Rules

Maxi and our numerous outdoor cats had reached a mutual non-aggression pact. They generally just avoided each other. There was one exception: Patches. Patches was a relatively small grey cat, who had decided that she was in charge, and should decide—or dictate—who was allowed on our deck. The deck extended across the back of our house, with a stairway leading up to it. The stairway was eight feet wide and was the point of access for Maxi and the cats. We'd often sit on the deck and Patches, the self-appointed guard of the deck, selected those who were allowed on it. Her list did not include Maxi.

Although Maxi was a tough dog, for some reason, this little six or seven pound cat was able to control him. Maxi would sit at the bottom of the stairs and wait until Patches was distracted or until she deserted her post as guard of the stairway. When either of these things happened, Maxi would race past her and join the rest of us.

Chapter Eleven

The Pied Piper

Our property was bordered on two sides by a blacktopped road. In good weather, we would walk down the road to the end of the lake.

Although there was little traffic, Maxi and Spinner, for their safety, walked on leashes, with Maxi carrying his own leash alongside Spinner and me. Like the Pied Piper, we would collect a trail of followers. At least three or four cats would join us. Most often, Big Mama, Black Tail, Gee Gee and Patches were part of our parade. Passing traffic would slow down and sometimes stop to check this unusual procession.

When we returned, we'd often go down to the dock where I would read, the dogs would watch the fish, and the cats stopped short of the dock. Sometimes Spinner's ever-present tennis ball would end up in the water. Since Spinner disliked getting wet, Maxi was the one who would retrieve the ball. Maxi would leap from the dock, swim to the ball and bring it back to the dock. Often it seemed to become a game, with Spinner deliberately dropping the ball into the water and Maxi jumping in to get it.

These idyllic days of summer always had their share of rain-filled days and the rain was often accompanied by impressive displays of lightning and booming thunder. Add "thunder" to the list of things Maxi feared, along with killer trucks and beheading bridges.

The only dog I've ever seen that wasn't afraid of thunder was Spinner. For him, thun-

der was not a cause for mindless fear as it was for Maxi, who could not be consoled during a thunderstorm.

One night, during a house-rattling thunderstorm, I went into the garage to spend some time with Maxi. My role of "Comforter" had been usurped. I found my husband and Maxi sharing Maxi's bed.

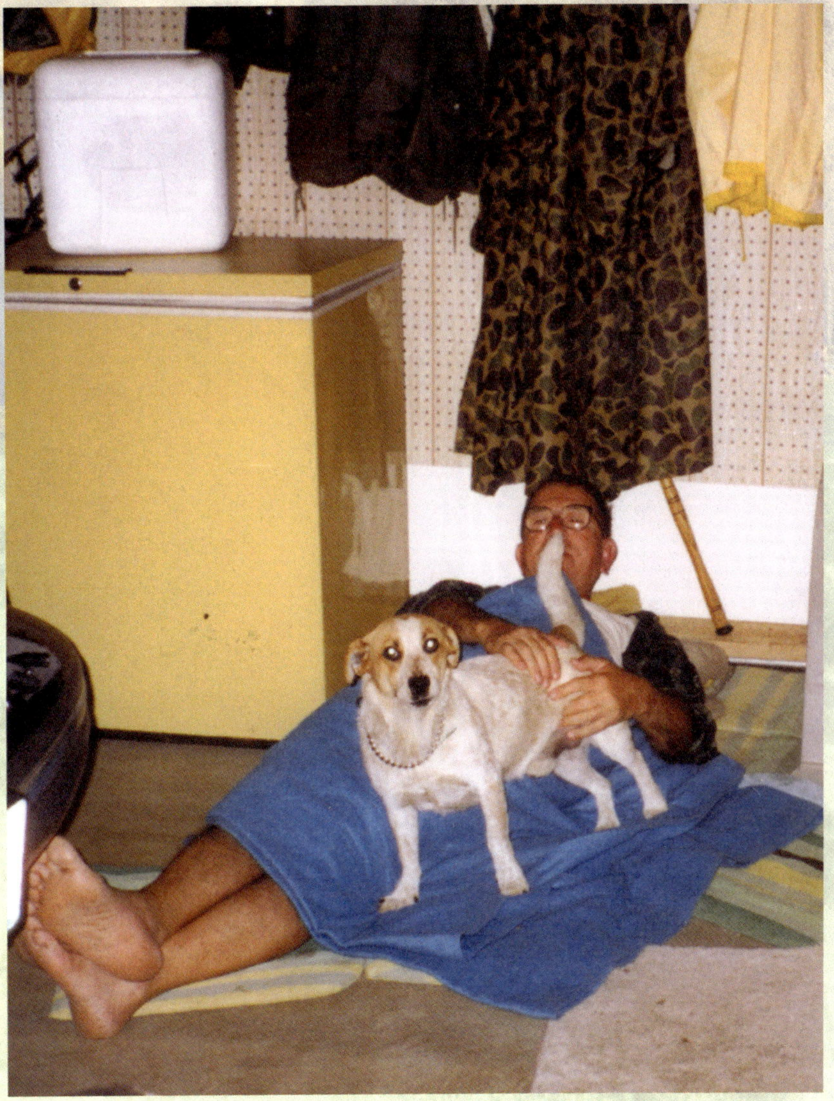

CHAPTER TWELVE

The Final Chapter

Although this is Maxi's story, it is also our story, my husband's and mine. For 10 years, we lived an idyllic life with our own spring-fed pond surrounded by cats, dogs, and other animals and birds. It was the kind of life I'd dreamed about as a child.

When I look back over this time, I often wonder about the person who dropped Maxi off on our country road. How could someone who had a wonderful dog like Maxi for two years just drop him off during the freezing nights of early March? Could they have a health problem, so that they could no longer keep him? Were they moving to a place that didn't allow dogs? Or what could Maxi's crime have been to warrant his lonely exile? Collecting shoes? Playing tug-of-war, sometimes with socks that didn't survive the game?

In any case, the pleasure that Maxi added to our lives was like winning the lottery. … And I'm very certain that from Maxi's viewpoint, he also held a winning ticket.

Maxi's Game
MAXI
PATCHES CARDS
39
40
41
42
43
44
45
46
47
48
49
50
51
52
53
54
55
56
59
60
61
62
63
64
65
66
67
68
69
70
71

Start
1
2
3
4
5
6
7
8
9
10
11
12
13
14
15
16
17
18
19
20
21
22
23
24
25
26
27
28
29
30
31
32
33
34
35
36
37
38

Maxi's Game

How to Play

2-5 Players

- Players select a token using it to move along Maxi's footprints.
- Players throw one die to determine who begins with high score beginning.
- Players throw the die and move the number shown on the die.
- Players landing on Patches, the cat; read the question and follow the directions.

- If they lose a turn, they will have to forfeit.
- Players landing on Maxi get a 2nd turn.

The first player to read Maxi's house wins the game.
To reach Maxi's house, the exact number must be thrown.

Take a trip to the Vet—skip a Turn
Take a Walk around the Lake go to #55

Take an Extra Turn.
Patches is in the Pied Piper Parade

Tap a Nap! My jobs are not Easy.
—Lose a turn.

Someone is coming in the driveway.
—Go to #10 to meet them.

What good Luck! Patches is Taking a
Break —Advance 2 spaces

Take a Break to Play a Game of
Hide the Shoes. —Go to #15

Someone came to Fish.
—Go to #48 and Bark.

Patches is Blocking the Path
—Go back 7 spaces

My favorite visitor From Chicago
Arrived. Treats —Go to #9

Patches is Blocking the Path
—Go back 7 spaces.

Uncle Bill came to visit—
—Go to space #15

Help in the Garden. Dig holes. Dig
big holes. —Lose a turn.

Patches is coming
Move forward 3 spaces.

Spinner reports The Moles are Busy
again. —Go to #25 to hunt them!

There's a puppy in the mailbox.
—Go help at #2!

Play a game of Tug-of-War with
Spinner. —Lose a turn.

"Boom" Thunder
—Hide And Skip a turn.

What good Luck! Patches is taking a break —Advance 2 spaces.

Help Spinner get his ball out of the lake. —Go to #45

Help Spinner hunt those Pesky Moles. —Go to #28

I've misplaced a Bone.
—Go to #32 to hunt for it.

Patches is Taking a Nap.
—Move forward 4 spaces.

Time for a lesson in Car Riding.
—Lose a turn.

Sit on the deck to watch the Sunrise.
—Lose a turn.

Hot weather –Time for a Swim.
—Go to #48.

Join the Pied Piper's Parade.
—Go to #15.

Line up at #35 to be combed.